PEACE

GOD'S WORD

RELIGIOUS COLORING BOOK

HE LIVES

By: Sylvie Cyr

ARCHWAY PUBLISHING

Scripture taken from the King James Version of the Bible.

Archway Publishing books may be ordered through booksellers or by contacting:

Archway Publishing
1663 Liberty Drive
Bloomington, IN 47403
www.archwaypublishing.com
1 (888) 242-5904

ISBN: 978-1-4808-5282-2 (sc)
ISBN: 978-1-4808-5283-9 (e)

Print information available on the last page.

Archway Publishing rev. date: 04/10/2018

The Lord is
my Shepherd;
I shall not want

PSALMS 23:1

11

I AM THE
Good Shepherd;
I KNOW MY SHEEP
&
MINE KNOW
ME.

Safe in his
Arms

Our
Father
who
art in Heaven
Hallowed be
Thy name

His love fills the
World with light

Give us this day "OUR DAILY BREAD." MATT 6:11

HE LIVES

HE'S THE LILY OF THE VALLEY.

Our FATHER,
WHO art in
heaven,
HaLLoWED bE
ThY Name, tHY
Kingdom come,
thy will Be done,
ON EartH as it is iN
heaveN! ♡
AMEN.

MATT
6:9-10

THis IS THE DAY WHICH THE LORD HAS MADE LET US REJOICE AND BE GLAD IN IT.

PSALM 118:24

Sing to the
Lord a
New
Song

Psalms 96:1

Born in a Manger

IN A MANGER

THE WISEMEN

THE SHEPHERDS

FLIGHT TO EGYPT

THE CARPENTER

43

ENTERING JERUSALEM

"JESUS AND THE CHILDREN

IN THE TEMPLE

HEALING THE SICK

FEEDING THE MULTITUDE

IN THE GARDEN

THE I AST SUPPER

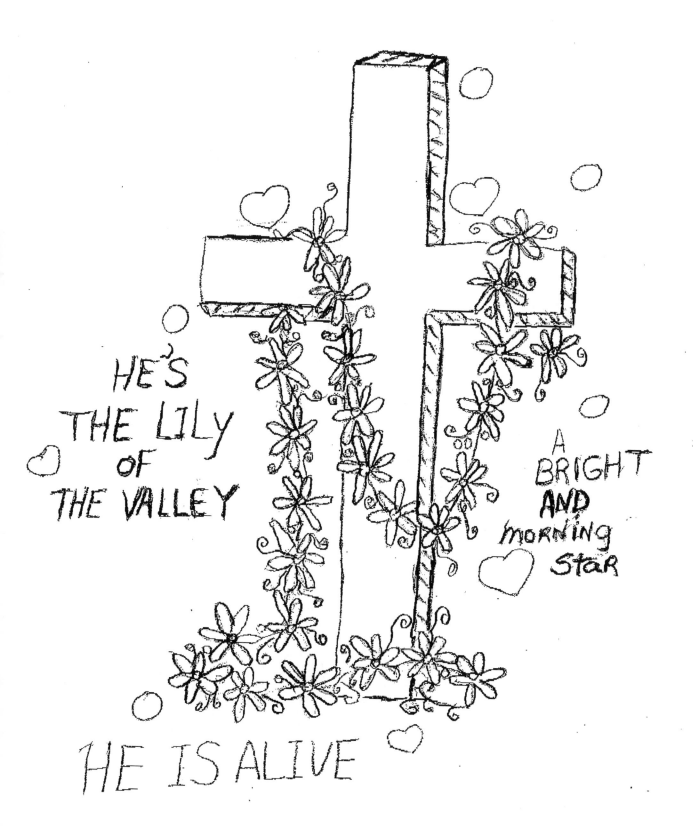

HE'S
THE LILY
OF
THE VALLEY

A
BRIGHT
AND
morning
Star

HE IS ALIVE

"HE IS RISEN"

THE ASCENSION

All things are possible with God

Mark - 10:27

Lilies

Thy WORD IS a Light unto my feet and a Lamp unto my path

Psalms 119:105

He makes Everything
Beautiful in his
own Way—Sin its Time...
Eccl. 3:11

The Cross

Made the Difference for Me...

Fruit of
the Spirit

Live by the Spirit...

Love,
Joy,
Peace,
Patience,
Kindness,
Goodness,
Faithfulness,
Gentleness,
and

Self-Control....

Gal: 5:22
Eph: 5:09

Prayer is the Key to Heaven, But... Faith unlocks the door.

As for
me
and my
House
○   we will
serve the
Lord ♡

Joshua 24:15,
PSALMS 91:9,10.

○   if you make
the most high your
dwelling ....
then no harm will
befall you,
No disaster will
come near your
tent.

79

Printed in the United States
By Bookmasters